IN EXTREMIS

Neil Bartlett

IN EXTREMIS

A Love Letter

OBERON BOOKS
LONDON

First published in 2000 by Oberon Books Ltd.
(incorporating Absolute Classics)
521 Caledonian Road, London N7 9RH
Tel: 020 7607 3637 / Fax: 020 7607 3629

e-mail: oberon.books@btinternet.com

A catalogue record for this book is available from the British
Library.

ISBN: 1 84002 205 1

Cover design: Humphrey Gudgeon
Front cover photograph of Corin Redgrave rehearsing *In
Extremis* by Mark Douet
Back cover photograph: *Oscar Wilde*, by Napoleon Sarony, 1882
(courtesy of the National Portrait Gallery, London)
Typography: Richard Doust

Printed in Great Britain by Antony Rowe Ltd, Reading.

Contents

Writing Wilde: In Extremis

Neil Bartlett

My text, commissioned by Corin Redgrave as a companion-piece to his solo rendition of Wilde's *De Profundis*, is spun from a single historical fact. According to a telegram sent the next morning to his dear friend Ada Leverson, on the night of March 24, 1895, just one week before the beginning of the trial that was to cost him his reputation, his liberty, his home, his family and quite soon his life, Oscar Wilde went to visit a society palm-reader called Mrs Robinson. She read his palm, and told him that the trial would be a great triumph.

The next day a gathering of his friends made a last-ditch attempt to persuade him to flee London for the safety of France; he refused. The rest is a history we're still living through.

We can never know what actually happened that night. But the story is too good to let lie; it might possibly hold a vital clue to the fascinating, appalling story of Wilde's downfall. We want to know why this famous man, with his brilliant mind and no less astonishing address book, turned, on that night of all nights, to a palm-reader. And why, as his letter to Ada Leverson and his behaviour the next day indicate, did he believe her? It seems profoundly irrational. We must not, however, let hindsight blind us to the fact that Wilde was faced with an impossible situation. Was he to leave Lord Alfred Douglas, the man with whom he was so deeply, disastrously in love? Leave his two young sons, whom he adored? Wilde was right in *De Profundis* to speak of the madness, the near-insanity of what happened to him. What place was there for reason in the city which had so suddenly turned against him? In less than three months an unholy alliance of media hostility, class prejudice and homophobic hatred had transformed Wilde from a darling celebrity into the worst kind of criminal pervert. A palmist might claim to decipher the madness as well as anyone.

But surely he knew, as he set out in a cab to meet her, that Mrs Robinson was a charlatan? She had after all read his palm once before, at a society party. She'd played the oldest trick in the book; predicting foreign travel (hardly an unlikely event given Douglas's penchant for making Wilde pay for frequent trips abroad). Perhaps that was her appeal; Wilde loved charlatans, if a charlatan is someone who makes lying not only a profession, but an art. His heroes and heroines are in this sense all liars; they make truth a performance. It is no accident that *De Profundis*, which of all his writings is the only one concerned to tell and prove the truth, is also his greatest *tour de force* performance, it's great outpouring of hate and love rehearsed for months in the solitude of Reading Gaol.

By way of explanation for his apparent passivity in the face of imminent disaster, Wilde is often said to have been deeply superstitious, to have believed that his destruction was somehow inevitable. Perhaps that's why he went to Mrs. Robinson that night. Certainly, his work is always haunted by the idea of Fate, of Doom. All of his heroes are marked by destiny; Earnest was destined to marry Gwendolen from the moment Miss Prism left her handbag in the cloakroom at Victoria Station; Dorian was doomed from the moment he voiced the wish that his picture might age while he might not. Bizarrely, Wilde's own fiction even seems sometimes to predict with fatalistic accuracy his own destiny; Lord Arthur Savile, in a short story written eight years before Wilde met Mrs Robinson, becomes a criminal precisely because of his superstitious belief in the predictions of a palmist who he meets at a party.

*

I have invented very little. I have adopted Wilde's own technique of redeploying phrases, cadences and even whole speeches from one work in another. I have stolen from fiction – the fee of one hundred guineas, the names of the duchesses, the tear-stained walk through London at dawn are all from *Lord Arthur Savile's Crime*, for instance – and given new meanings to details lifted from letters and interviews. Like all good charlatans, I can claim to have stuck to the facts; Mrs Robinson did indeed provide advice to several M.P.s, and she did publish a photographically illustrated manual of palm-reading (*The Graven Palm*, Edward Arnold, London, 1911); and she did live just round the corner from two friends of Wilde called Alfred and Charlie, a couple who he referred to as "married". He did wear lemon yellow gloves and a scarab ring, and a coat with a beaver collar; he did pay a well-publicised visit to a performance of *The Importance of Being Earnest* accompanied by both his wife and his lover. I have not invented Wilde's terror, or his love, or the details of his love-life. He already knew on March 24th that Queensberry's lawyers had obtained copies of his love-letters to Lord Alfred Douglas; but he didn't yet know that they had traced ten of the young men who he had paid to have sex with either Douglas or himself in the previous three years. And, yes, London was, that terrible spring, freezing; on the night that *The Importance of Being Earnest* opened, the Serpentine carried six inches of ice.

But as for this version of the story being "true"…well; no truth can be separated from the circumstances of its telling. A hundred years after his death, we find other truths in Wilde's life and work than those found when he swore to tell the truth ,the whole truth and nothing but the truth in the dock at the Old Bailey. We flatter ourselves that we read his story very differently to the jury who found him guilty, or to the newspaper editors who boosted their circulation on the back of lurid, moralising editorials, or to all those who approved of or revelled in his humiliation. We've put up a statue, given him a plaque in Westminster Abbey, adopted him as an icon, claimed him as a pioneer, studied him to death, republished him endlessly and made him one the very few above-the-title box office guarantee names of our entertainment industry. But I do not think we have understood him yet, or what was done to him. I don't think we realise how much he is with us, rather than behind us.

Of all the details of this story, one image has stuck in my mind; Wilde and Mrs Robinson sitting alone in her room, silent, unobserved in the middle of a London night noisy with speculation, rumour and libel, the smug applause of theatres, the vicious gossip of hotel dining rooms. What I wanted to do was the impossible thing that only theatre can do; to put us in that room.

*

With regards to staging; I am writing this introduction before the opening night of the first production, so I've no idea what the piece will finally look like. As I indicate in the script, my intention was that it be put on stage without any token "period" clutter, and most especially without any realistic depiction of Mrs. Robinson's room. I had in mind a rather sombre, beautiful space, with the audience close around it, with just two mahogany chairs; a space where the actors would feel free to talk directly to the audience and also to move whenever and however they needed to. I would emphasise *beautiful*, despite the suggestion of a resonant emptiness; this is Oscar Wilde, after all.

This piece is respectfully dedicated to the two great actors for whom I had the privilege of writing it, Sheila Hancock and Corin Redgrave.

Neil Bartlett
September 2000

Characters

Oscar Wilde

Mrs Robinson, a palm-reader

In Extremis was first performed at the Cottesloe Theatre on 3 November 2000, in tandem with Wilde's *De Profundis*. It was also performed on the night of 30 November 2000, exactly one hundred years after Wilde's death. The cast was as follows:

W, Corin Redgrave

R, Sheila Hancock

Director, Trevor Nunn

Think of a rather sombre, beautiful space,
more or less empty.

There are two chairs, facing each other, some good
distance apart.

They often say things the other doesn't hear.

There is a letter on the floor by her chair.
This is the only prop.

In this script, R = Mrs Robinson, W = Oscar Wilde.

Perhaps:

She is sitting in a chair facing another empty chair.

We hear the sound of a clock ticking.

*He enters. He sits, facing her, and.............
says nothing.*

She suspends the ticking of the clock with a small gesture –

R

There were only two people in the room that evening; and both of us are now dead.

And since no one else was in the room that night, if you want to know what he said – the actual words that he used – and that I used – well; I'm the only one who can tell you.

That is why you've come, isn't it? To hear him. To hear what he really said.

Of course a lot of things weren't actually said, out loud – much of that evening will have to be inferred, deduced. How can we ever really know what a man is or was thinking, you may say. Interpretation, fortunately, is my profession.

She looks at him, and us.

People often come to hear me speak and they sit there and I can tell what they're thinking, they're thinking, its all nonsense really, isn't it, really, palm-reading, I mean how do I know she's not just making it all up – not that that ever stops them paying to come and hear me. I can see it in their faces, "I shan't believe you, whatever you say."

Sometimes they even come right out and say it, they say, Mrs. Robinson, are you lying? And do you know, I always give them the same answer. Am I lying? No.

She looks at him again.

It's extraordinary to think of him now. Dead, I mean. And so quickly, too. Such a big man, he was. Seemed to be.

Anyway...........

That evening, after he'd gone, I wrote a letter, to.....a friend. Someone rather well known. Forgive me if I refer to it now, but I do want to get the details right. Details, as he once said to me, are the only things that really interest.

Reading.

53 Mortimer St. West One

March 24th.

My dear,

I felt I must write, as much for my sake as yours: I am eager to preserve an accurate account of my most recent consultation, and also should not like to think of you or anyone else hearing of it first in the papers.

You will surely never guess who I received as a client late here this evening. Mr Wilde. Under the present circumstances, too! I have of course met him before, in January, at that last evening of Lady Narborough's – you may recall the unfortunate incident of my telling Lady Fermor right out before everyone that she did not care a bit for music but was extremely fond of musicians.

It is so gratifying when a client is encouraged to return for a second reading. He doubtless recalled my success on the earlier occasion – I foresaw an imminent journey, and was quite right; he told me he had received tickets from Thomas Cook only hours prior to the party. You may have read of the trip in the St James Gazette last month. Algiers, I believe.

I cannot of course reveal what transpired on this occasion but I can only say that he seemed to me most satisfied, and left evidently content. I am glad for him. Tomorrow I am at Lady Merton's and shall doubtless hear more of how the case is expected to proceed. It starts on Monday week, does it not? Shall you go?

Did I tell you by the way that the Duchess of Monmouth has introduced me to Lord Leighton, President of the Royal Academy? A most distinguished hand.

Believe me your affectionate friend,

– and so on.

Referring to the letter.

.......the 24th of March. 189.....5. I'd forgotten I met him twice. I wonder what time it was? – ....late,
I think......

Laying it down.

I should have kept a copy really – papers are so useful. So useful should any verification of what was said be required at a later date; hindsight, unlike foresight, is such an approximate art. And sceptics abound. Not everyone is as persuaded of my powers as the dear Duchess of Berwick, who so obligingly wrote in my book of testimonials after I had read her hand: "Mrs Robinson seemed able to recall my past more accurately than I could have done myself". Some are sceptical, some anxious, some think it not quite right. But then, as Lady Merton said when she introduced me to Lady Lancing, nothing interesting ever is.

Oh dear, I'm starting to talk like him. You see he was so very......infectious. In his manner.

For several years it was quite the style to talk like him. Or to imagine that one could.

1895. What a very long time ago. And what a very difficult year.

I liked number fifty three. It was a very effective room; conducive. I received clients from all the most distinguished walks of life there – painters, musicians, novelists, celebrities of the stage; journalists, eminent judges – KCs. Several MPs. The traffic did of course necessitate rather heavy drapery, but I like that. A little peace and quiet and rather a lot of maroon plush never does any harm in my line of business; quiet.....hush..... and a very careful positioning of the lamps. Nothing too harsh, to interrogatory. They're quite nervous enough as it is, most of them. He wasn't, of course. Of course I like them to be nervous;

nerves are very good, very good for making people grateful, making them appreciative of the gift. That's why I invariably make them wait. Worry. Sweat – you'd be surprised how many of them sweat. Dry palm, wet palm, it can tell you a great deal about a person.

He was good at nerves.

Pause.

Dear Mr Wilde, I said, I'm so sorry to have kept you waiting, please do come in – we shook hands – and please do forgive me but since I received your card I have been in *such* – he was lucky I agreed to see him at that short notice, actually, or indeed at all at that time of night. In those days, people – and I mean very distinguished people – had to wait weeks, weeks for an appointment, and I was very strict in my hours, private consultations from ten until four only – unless of course I was booked for a more public function in the evening. As I very often was. In those days.

"Most urgently", it said on his card. In his books men seem constantly to be flinging themselves onto sofas with cries of despair but when he came to see me I can only report that he sat down, and stayed there. He sat well, though. Large man, as I said. The way he was dressed you'd have thought I was a photographer; a beautiful dark ten-button jacket, satin lapels. A beaver collar on his greatcoat.... His tie was gold, a dark gold, with a pearl pin. You might think it odd that I can remember all that, but I do. I notice. It's part of my job.

Of course if I told you it was a coral pin, and a lavender tie – you'd believe me.

Lemon yellow gloves – he took one off to light a cigarette – and the most marvellous hands. Always so....arranged. Composed. And the most marvellous ring, most unusual for a gentleman, a scarab.

He did smoke incessantly.

And I noticed, when he lit his cigarette, his right hand, shaking – only slightly.

She looks at him; beat.

Oh Mr Wilde I said I do hope you don't find the room too dark I find that for a good reading privacy is essential, and drapes do create a sense of privacy, in modern life atmosphere counts for so much don't you think, privacy has become especially precious to me of late, in recent years I have often denied myself the pleasure of accepting invitations so as not to be obliged to parade my gift as merely one fashionable curiosity amidst a crowd of others, though I did positively badger our mutual friend Lady Narborough to have me at her last reception as I simply couldn't bear to think that I had passed two whole seasons without ever having met you, having followed your work with such pleasure.

He says nothing.

And having heard so much news of you.

Beat.

As has most of London.

Nothing.

The successes, the appearances at the most distinguished addresses, the beautiful house in Chelsea –

The happy home life........

Still he does not respond.

Are you quite comfortable Mr Wilde I said.

Yes he said, he was; he said Oh most comfortable Mrs Robinson. Almost at peace, in fact. But then I have always felt most comfortable on the fringes of Society, and when one is this far north of Oxford Street one might almost be in the country.

Still he does not respond.

I understand that the opening at the St James's was a great triumph, I said – I was unable to join Lady Herkomer in her box that night, sadly – though I have of course attended since, I said, I thought our dear Miss Leclerq especially fine, but then she so often is. I said. I had heard you declined to make a speech, – which surprised me when I read it in The Times, as he was not usually so retiring – he was at that period in his career very, *very* accomplished in the arts of publicity – Mr Wilde, I said; it has always looked to me as if it gave you very great pleasure to appear before the curtain –

W

It gives me none whatsoever.

R

He said.

W

No artist finds any interest in seeing his public. The public is however very much interested in seeing the artist. Personally, I prefer the French custom, according to which the name of the dramatist is simply announced to the public by the oldest actors in the piece.

R

Would you prefer to have it done like that in London?, I said.

W

Certainly, I said. The more the public is interested in artists, the less it is interested in art. The personality of the artist is not a thing the public should know anything about.

> *Pause.*

It might be more interesting if the name of the author were announced by the *youngest* actor present.

> *Pause.*

What keen interest you take, Mrs Robinson, in the most delicate crises of an artist's life. Stepping out from behind a curtain to face a packed house of Englishmen baying one's name does require a certain courage. It is only in deference to such an imperious mandate that I consent to expose myself. I would have spoken – the public has always been so appreciative of my work that I feel *felt* it would be a pity to spoil its evening – but certain of my friends advised me against it.

I find I prefer at the moment quiet evenings, quiet entertainments – such as yourself –

R

Mr Wilde why are you here?

Pause.

W

Because I find myself in trouble of a very particular kind, and in need of advice. Friends, especially close ones, are so bad at this sort of thing.... I am sure you cannot be the only woman in London who has not read the painfully accurate accounts of my social and professional life which appear with such remarkable frequency in the Times, the St James Gazette, the Pall Mall Gazette, The Daily Chronicle, and even, I am told, in the Illustrated London News.

R

Well, I had read – as I am sure you have – about his being asked to leave the hotel in Monte Carlo, with Lord Alfred Douglas and of course about Lord Queensbury and the charge, the libel, but –

I didn't know.

None of us knew.

So I said, No, I've heard nothing. Or rather, I never believe half of what I hear, Mr. Wilde.

W

How wise you are not to do that Mrs Robinson. Everything is so adulterated these days that even rumour can hardly be got in a pure condition.

R

But what makes a man of your reputation come to call on me?

W

Do you know, I nearly didn't. I nearly told the driver to pass your door and turn left into Fitzroy Street, number 46, but then I remembered someone saying that Fred and Charlie have gone away. Mrs Robinson forgive me for speaking as plainly as a character from the pen of one our more popular dramatists but you see I need someone to talk to. I can't talk to Robbie, I've tried that. I have talked to Robbie far too much, far too often, and I don't care for what he tells me. I can hardly talk to my wife – I can hardly bear to be in the same house as my wife, her downstairs, me upstairs, and both of us creeping. I don't dare talk to a priest, much as I should like to sit in the shadows and whisper obscenities to a grave young man who knows nothing of my life. And Cyril, my darling Cyril, to whom I tell all my best stories, the only one who truly understands me, was asleep. Like the good boy he is. So here, Mrs Robinson, I am.

I didn't say that. How wonderful if I had. What I said was; Oh I think everyone should have their hands told at least once a month, so as to know what not to do. Of course one will do it all the same, but it is so pleasant to be warned. A really stern warning can make even the slightest error of judgement feel like the most marvellous act of folly.

Pause.

R

He sat there, smoking, and I had absolutely no idea what he was thinking. Usually I can tell, or guess – it's half the art;....but with him, I had no idea.

W

Christ but it's cold this spring, bitter.

R

I knew what he wanted, though. The same as they all wanted; the impossible.

Shall we do it then, I said.

He said.

W

Yes.

Just before we begin Mrs Robinson, I should warn you that I am not unaccustomed to the ways of charlatans. Indeed I regularly provide employment for some of the most accomplished charlatans in London, albeit those working in a profession somewhat different to your own.

R

I presume you refer to the theatre, Mr Wilde.

W

I do. To some of the best theatre in London.

R

You are not the first client who has wondered whether I am merely an impostor, and my consultations merely performance. Indeed, the most common question I am asked is, am I lying. I can only give you the answer I always give.

W

Which is?

R

No. Would you take off your other glove, please.

Before the reading itself, we hear Mrs Robinson's (well-rehearsed) short lecture guide to The Art of Palmistry.

Palmistry is perhaps the most ancient of all the arts of divination, having been practised by both the Chaldeans and the Hindoo. It is certainly one that has seen a great revival of popularity in these uncertain and difficult times.

Though it is as yet an inexact one, Palmistry is also a science. Some hands read like a well-printed history; some like a faulty edition read by inefficient light; a very few present the difficulties of an hieroglyphic papyrus to which the Egyptologist has as yet no key. Yet all are capable of analysis; patient and *systematic* observation and interpretation will decipher even the most obscure destiny. To this end, a thorough knowledge of the system is essential. It may be briefly summarised as follows – I would refer those of you interested in pursuing the subject further to my popular photographically illustrated manual "The Graven Palm", Edward Arnold, publishers – ; firstly General Characteristics (as tabulated in my second chapter) may be deduced from the overall topography of the palm itself and from the shape and arrangement of the fingers; then Specific Histories and Future Incidents of the life may be read from the Lines. The lines are five in number: The Line of the Heart, the Line of the Head, the Line of Fortune and Fame, the Line of Health and The Line of Life, also referred to as those of Venus, Jupiter, Saturn, Mars, and Mercury.

When predictions are being made it is most important it be made clear to the client that there is nothing inevitable in any events of the life which depend upon our own personal actions and efforts. In regards to a man's character, only the past is certain; the future is at best only probable. The palm-reader must also at all times be aware of variety of expectation; remember that a line indicating a great advance in life may indicate preferment to a bishopric or a superior position in a provincial bank, according to the possessor of the hand. Tact, and an infinite sympathy with the circumstances, foibles and sins of others, are prerequisites.

Do not be surprised by any subterfuge on the part of the client. Well-known Society ladies, even personalities of the stage, not infrequently come and see me wearing full length black crepe veils, so as to conceal their identities and remove any possibility of my predictions being based on prior knowledge of their lives. Remember also that people reveal themselves precisely in their disguises. A married woman who has removed her wedding ring reveals her hopes for the future as clearly as a veiled celebrity her longings for anonymity.

He chose the cleverest disguise; ostentation.

I prefer to sit close to the client, facing him. Other cheiromantists recommend sitting to the client's side, so that both subject and reader may have the same view of the hand. Personally I do not advocate any attempt to view another's life from their perspective; one should trust one's own.

Take the hand in a decisive but reassuring grip. Spread the palm fully, bending the fingers back firmly if necessary.

Which I did.

Warm..............surprisingly warm.

Pause.

W

What did you see?

A longer pause.

I am waiting, Mrs Robinson.

R

We are all waiting, Mr Wilde – obvious, like the silence – but, like the silence, effective.

It was a sensual hand. Sensual and selfish. I commented on his ring –

W

I have the superstitious nature of my race. The delightful boy who sold it me assured me that it would bring me bad luck always; I am happy to say that its powers have turned out to be entirely genuine.

Pause.

I trust your silence is a sign my hand is unusually hard to read. I should so hate, at this late juncture of my career, to be told that I had become obvious. Indeed I have always held that incomprehension is the sincerest form of flattery.

R

Mr Wilde, please listen very carefully to what I am going to say.

I see no cancer, madness, death by drowning or violent death by accident in your hand.

You are too impulsive in your enthusiasms.

You feel deeply the appeal of the material.

You have no fondness for the outdoor life.

You have a desire to obtain pleasure and amusement at any cost or hazard.

I see great ability. Arrogance.

Steadfastness.

Notoriety.

W

Blackmail?

R

No.

Great Courage.

Decency.

Generosity.

W

Thank you. Would you care for a cigarette?

R

I declined.

    Beat.

You are not always sincere with those you love.

He said nothing.

You have not yet achieved all that you hope to.

    Beat.

He said nothing.

If I see doubt or mistrust in a client's face,
especially this early in a reading, then I pause,

turn the hands towards the lamp, peer more closely, pause again and then tell them something entirely obvious. "You are swayed by the opinions of others more often than you would like."; they will more often than not blench with recognition, as if I had divined something they imagined they had concealed from even those nearest to them. Trust is restored.

Of course, you're thinking, you would never fall for that. You would probably never have come to me in the first place. You're not the sort of person that would ever need to. And if you ever did – just suppose – well you'd know at once what was going on....... Funny; I don't even need to see your hand. I can tell just by looking at you....... You are not always sincere with those you love. You have not yet achieved all that you once hoped to. Have you?

Please don't be shocked at my divulging the minor tricks of my profession. That's how you can be sure I'm dead, by the way. Only the dead give up all their secrets.

She looks at him.

W

What else?

R

Nicotine, and a writer's callous on the right index finger.

W

How marvellous of you to have deduced the two principle occupations of my life.

31

R

These are the hands of a very charming man.

W

Charm, like wit, is a myth invented by handsome people to account for the peculiar social success of the ugly.

R

You have considerable powers of attraction.

W

Fortunately it is only unsuitable people who find me attractive.

R

You have many friends, but do not always trust their advice.

W

Advice, like pleasure, should always be paid for. Only strangers can give it.

R

You are sometimes profligate.

W

In the sphere of finance, as in the sphere of morality, my credit would seem to be unlimited.

R

You are vain.

W

I am glad to hear it. To be perfect would leave no room for development.

R

You are prone to dreams –

W

Society often forgives the criminal, but never the dreamer. / I –

R

But disinclined to feed on dreams.

W

How wrong you are; I am sure I obtain more nourishment from the fantasies of the brain than I ever do from Boulestin or even Kettner's.

R

You wear a mask.

W

It is not wise to show one's heart to the world.

R

The world and you are on very good terms.

Beat.

W

Civility is invariably a prelude to insult.

Beat.

R

You are sensitive to insult.

W

I have indeed been abused by telegram and by letter, not mention the immense opportunities afforded by the open postcard; in unsigned articles, as well as in those most illustriously signed; by the glittering gaslight of public dining rooms no less than by the bald daylight of Kensington High Street; in the Cafe Royal, and in Swan and Edgars. I have even been most elaborately insulted in my own library. Your insight into my character is all I expected it to be, Mrs Robinson; really you may leave that to the expert, myself. I am chiefly interested in the future. I want you to tell my fortune. You do tell fortunes?

R

And misfortunes.

Beat.

W

I am not afraid.

R

Good. The Lines are five; those of the Heart, of the Head, of Fortune and Fame, of Health, and of Life itself. These lines contain the possible, the probable, and also the certain.

W

And is no escape possible?

R

In regard to a man's character, only the past is certain; the future is at best only probable.

W

I am so glad to hear there is some uncertainty left in modern life.

R

There is nothing inevitable in any events of the life which depend upon our own personal actions and efforts. Clear distinctions must / be drawn –

W

Why *am* I here? Sitting in this very ordinary room with a very ordinary woman – why is it by the way that people never look in life as they do in fiction , it is so predictable of them – quite desperate for her to tell me what to do. Longing for a paid fool to speak to me and say kind words. Really, if that was what I wanted, I could have got that at number 46.

How she talks.

R

– the line of Venus, the line of the Heart.

W

Perhaps Fred and Charlie will be in later.

R

The Mount of Venus is prominent, –

W

Perhaps they'll introduce me to someone *new*.

R

And the girdle is deeply cut. The Meridian, or Line, is –

W

The line, frankly, is immaterial!

Pause.

Do forgive me. Nowadays quoting my lines is so fashionable I am told even the young men in my latest play do it. And if I may be allowed the luxury of quoting myself again, this time in the character of my poor dear flustered Lady Windermere, what I want are details, details are the only things that interest. What is going to happen to me? In view of the lateness of the hour, / I said –

R

/ I said Mr Wilde, allow me a quotation. "Though it is as yet an inexact one, Palmistry is a science. Patient and *systematic* observation and interpretation will decipher even the most obscure Destiny".

Shall we proceed?

W

Very well.

R

Thank you.

The Line of the Heart. The line is deep and strong.

> *Beat.*

W

Is it?

R

I see only one marriage.

W

That is I believe the fashionable number.

R

And with regard to its future I suggest you take a hansom back to Chelsea and ask your wife. I feel sure she'll tell you.

I should have said.

But I didn't. Of course I didn't. I said:

The two lines end almost together.

I didn't see that, but that's what I said. It's what most people want to hear – that "almost" covers more or less every eventuality. As it happens, I was right, more or less; she died eighteen months before he did.

I saw them "together", once.

Yes, I saw you at the theatre, the two of you. Pretty girl. You'd got her dressed up in cinnamon velvet, with white fur – god it was cold that spring, bitter – and her face was as white as a sheet. Sitting there completely silent while the rest of the theatre roared. When the two of you laughed, she flinched – yes, that's right, Douglas was sitting with them.......unbelievable, centre stalls, the whole dress circle leaned forward....the blondest hair I think I have ever seen.

Men like that are disgusting, they disgust me. Husbands who lie. Not that I knew – I didn't know, no one did. If I had known, if I had known whose hand I was holding – well, I am sure I would have read different things in it. I would have seen –

> *Beat.*

The Line of Travel. I see extensive travel in your future. But then you have always travelled.

W

Oh I have.

R

Widely.

W

Marvellously. Rome, Naples, Paris, Venice........;
Brighton.

R

America?

W

America.

R

Algiers.

W

Algiers indeed. How clever of you to remember
that Mrs Robinson.

R

Oh I see it quite clearly –

W

But she saw nothing. She knew nothing; she
understood nothing.

She never saw you wake up crying like a child for
more hashish. She never saw us followed by
lovely brown things from street to street, whole
villages peopled by fauns.

R

It is a wonderful country is it not?

W

Most wonderful. There is of course the problem of great poverty, but when the beggars have profiles that is so easily solved.

R

I think I should find the heat most trying.

W

The most beautiful of them was said by our guide to be deceitful; and indeed, he was. One memorable night he upset both Lord Alfred and myself quite awfully.

R

And of course the great inconvenience –

Beat.

– I think it must have been dreadful, not marvellous at all.

W

She saw nothing of our life these past two and a half years –

R

Trains, boats, taxis;

W

Never saw your beautiful letters waiting for me at my breakfast table, or mine in return to you;

R

– hotels, restaurants, other people's houses –

W

Never saw the flowers, or the jewels.

R

Never a moment's peace. Never a moment to sit down.

W

Our luncheons at the Berkley with Robbie, or alone; the idle, laughing afternoons, the splendid dinners, the charming suppers at Willis's, the drives home long after midnight.

R

Never any quiet.

W

Never saw the two of us reflected in the mirrors of the Savoy, or the shop windows of Bond Street; never watched us play the profligate amongst the easily bought, squandering my fortune on utterly splendid pleasures.

R

The successes, the appearances at the most distinguished addresses, –

W

Never saw you stretched out on a sofa.

R

The late hours, the stares, the chatter, the laughter.

W

Never saw you pay a boy with the diamonds from your dress shirt.

R

The applause.

W

Did you know that success becomes a habit? One's mind no less that one's body becomes accustomed to pleasure. And nowadays the only pleasure worth having, the one supreme pleasure worth knowing, the one joy one never tires of, is power, power over other men, power over the world. We are told that in our century only the rich possess it. But the fool, the fraud, and the liar have their own power. The lowest as the highest comedian has power. When I sat in my box at the St James theatre six weeks ago, and heard every man and woman in London who matters laughing at painted puppets who danced to my command, spoke blasphemies and indecencies of my devising, then I know Power, and the Pleasure of Power.

And what was once a great delicacy has now become my daily fare. Voices are raised against me of course. In England at least, no man can take his pleasures without attracting censure. But although my shame is a great luxury to me, an exquisite agony in which I indulge myself whenever I can, blame has no reality for me at all. Blame is a function of the narrow mind, and an operation of Society merely, whereas shame.... shame is a sensation. I do not blame myself for a single bottle needlessly ordered and left half drunk, a single dish left barely tasted. I do not blame myself for a single compliment accepted or young man's flattery enjoyed. I do not blame myself for a single cigarette, a single wasted evening, or a single kiss.

Pause.

R

I think he was very alone.

W

She has no idea. No one does.

R

The most talked-about man in London.

W

No one.

Go on.

R

Yes of course. The Line of Fortune is – broken....
You are not happy.

W

I have never sought happiness. I have sought
pleasure.

R

Have you found it?

W

Often. Mrs Robinson. Far too often. Do go on.

Pause.

Go on...

A silence, suddenly broken.

R

I saw something. Saw something, felt something –
no, saw something, saw him, weeping. Suddenly
much thinner and...weeping. I couldn't look at his
face, couldn't, / I bent over his hand –

W

/ She bent her head low over my hand, and was
silent, as if studying intently some mystery she
found there. I could hear the traffic, the dim roar
of London like the note of a distant organ.

/ She began to speak, but then –

R

/ I began to speak, but –

> *She thinks she hears someone in the*
> *audience.*

Did I what? Did I lie?

W

But then she –

R

No;

W

she faltered. / She said......

R

/ I said..........;

I see great success, great good fortune,

but then –

a wall. I'm sorry.

> *Pause.*

W

A wall that is built of marble or a wall that is made
of brick merely?

R

I spoke metaphorically.

45

W

Go on. If there is something written in my hand,
then tell me. Tell me what you saw there.

R

What makes you think I see anything more in
your hand, Mr Wilde, I said, anything more than
I have already told you –

W

I will pay you a hundred pounds.

Beat.

R

Guineas?

W

Certainly, I will send you the cheque tomorrow.

R

I got up and drew a heavy curtain across the door.
Usually I do that to frighten them, make them
think I am about to say something quite dreadful.
Only the fearful are grateful. But that night, I
remember, I remember needing time to think.

I sat down with him again, and took his hand.

Be quick, he said, be quick – as if I was a doctor
with a knife.

They know. They come to me clutching their own
disasters, their own deaths. Do you remember

how the people in his plays always – oh, no, you can't remember; you weren't there. How odd. The people in his plays used to talk all the time about "The Secret of Life". "The secret of life is never to have an emotion that is unbecoming." "The secret of life is to appreciate the pleasure of being terribly, terribly deceived." But the secrets they so long to hear are ones that they already know. Things they can't quite bring themselves to believe unless they've paid me to say them out loud.

I traced his Line of Fortune once more, very slowly, with my index finger, and I said –

> *He starts from the chair as if he cannot stand the pressure any longer, and after an agony of hesitation makes a move as if to exit. He stops with his back turned. Pause. He turns.*

> *Pause.*

Is there something you want to tell me, Mr Wilde?

Mr Wilde...............?

W

Mrs Robinson up until now I have contrived to an extraordinary degree to shield myself from the sordid perils of actual existence. I have lived a delicate and luxurious life. For the last two and a half years especially every detail of that life has been made marvellous, lavish, dazzling, the height of style. My mirrors have all been flattering ones, in the East End no less than in the West. I have been admired extravagantly. My very dress has made me an exemplar to the less fortunate. I have been the crown prince of joy, a Pierrot who knows not how to cry. I am, no less than my work is, specifically designed to create laughter out of the absurdity and cruelty of this our life. But on February the 28th at eleven o'clock I was standing in my club, the Albemarle, and the hall porter brought me a card with hideous words on it. Words which any gentleman or any member of the staff might have seen. Words for the world to look at. In consequence of which I am now engaged in a criminal prosecution. In consequence of which I feel myself assailed. Spilt on the sand. Fouled. In consequence of which I find myself in your room. Rather than dwell on the more fascinating mysteries of my personality and destiny, I should be so grateful if your art....or indeed, you..... might grant me some insight into rather more mundane matters.

In the matter of travel, for instance, am I to use the boat train in the near future? If I am, should I take the eleven o'clock, Chatham and Dover, or the seven o'clock to Newhaven, for Dieppe? You see I find myself obliged to take what my friend Mr Ross would probably call a horribly simple decision. Shall I stay, or shall I go?

R

Remember that I had no idea what was going to happen.

W

I long for certainty.

R

No one had.

W

And I *am* afraid of it.

R

No one ever does.

W

Whatever you have to say, say it without fear.
Don't say what you don't see, that is all.

Pause.

Tell me the truth.

Beat.

R

The truth, Mr Wilde, is rarely pure, and never
simple. Modern life –

W

A modern life, Mrs Robinson, is what I have
always wanted. It is the cost of such a life that I
need to know. What will happen if I stay?

Pause.

R

What I wanted to say was: I'm sorry. I'm so sorry.

/ But what I said was –

W

And what she said was –

the exact phrase I recall her using was –

R

I see a triumph. A very great triumph.

Beat.

W

And when she said that – / ah! – /

R

/ He heaved a / great sigh. Of relief.

W

Your name rose to my lips. Dear boy, dearest, my darling, my own golden-haired darling, you have been the whole beauty of life to me, and shall be again. You are everything to me. There have been moments when I thought it would be wiser to leave you – Ah! moments of weakness and madness! I can see you now, laughing. I can see you on the bed with Charlie and the boys, laughing. I can see you in the morning, with the sun behind you, making you all a glory of gilt and ivory. O my love, from your hair to your feet you are perfection to me. I love you, I love you, my heart is a rose!........ Love me always, always........always.

R

Did you say something, Mr Wilde?

W

Nothing of importance, Mrs Robinson.

R

He stood up, put on his gloves, said goodnight, and left.

W

As I walked home, my eyes were full of tears, for I knew I was safe. What route I took I hardly knew. I have a dim memory of wandering through a labyrinth of sordid streets, and it was dawn when I finally found myself in Piccadilly Circus. As I walked home to Chelsea I met some market workers on their way to Covent Garden. There was something in the dawn that seemed to me inexpressibly pathetic, and I thought of all the days that break in beauty, and that set in storm. They were laughing....what a strange London they see. How unreal. How like a strange dream. A London free from the sin of night and the smoke of day, a pallid, ghost-like city. I wondered what they thought of it, and what they knew of its splendour and its shame, of its fierce fiery-coloured joys, and its horrible hunger, of all it makes and mars from morn to eve. I envied them all that they did not know.

By the time I reached Tite Street the sky was a faint blue, and the birds were beginning to twitter in the gardens. It was too late to sleep, and I thought about you.

Perhaps he leaves.

R

When he was gone I put out the lamps and went to bed. A hundred guineas isn't bad for (*She looks at her watch and specifies the actual running time of the show.*) forty three minutes.

Now that both of us are dead, a hundred years dead, nobody can ever say for certain what happened in that room on Mortimer Street, on the evening of the twenty fourth of March, 1895. So listen very carefully to what I am going to say;

I told him I saw a great triumph.

The ticking of a clock . . .

Well, was I lying?

Slow fade to black.